THE WISH BOOK

Also by Alex Lemon

Fancy Beasts

Hallelujah Blackout

Happy: A Memoir

Mosquito

The WISH BOOK

ALEX LEMON

MILKWEED EDITIONS

Published 2014 by Milkweed Editions
Printed in Canada
Cover design by Stewart A. Williams
Cover photo/illustration by Stewart A. Williams
Author photo by Ariane Balizet
14 15 16 17   5 4 3 2
First Edition

Milkweed Editions, an independent nonprofit publisher, gratefully acknowledges sustaining support from the Bush Foundation; the Patrick and Aimee Butler Foundation; the Dougherty Family Foundation; the Driscoll Foundation; the Jerome Foundation; the Lindquist & Vennum Foundation; the McKnight Foundation; the voters of Minnesota through a Minnesota State Arts Board Operating Support grant, thanks to a legislative appropriation from the arts and cultural heritage fund, and a grant from the Wells Fargo Foundation Minnesota; the National Endowment for the Arts; the Target Foundation; and other generous contributions from foundations, corporations, and individuals. For a full listing of Milkweed Editions supporters, please visit www.milkweed.org.

Library of Congress Cataloging-in-Publication Data

Library of Congress Cataloging-in-Publication Data

Lemon, Alex.
[Poems. Selections]
The Wish Book : Poems / Alex Lemon. -- First Edition.
    pages cm
 Summary: "Offering unrestrained descriptions of sensory overload and tender meditations on fatherhood and mortality, these poems blur the nebulous line between the personal and the pop-cultural"-- Provided by publisher.
 ISBN 978-1-57131-450-5 (pbk. : acid-free paper) -- ISBN 978-1-57131-843-5 (e-book) (print)
 I. Title.
 PS3612.E468A6 2014
 811'.6--dc23
                              2013026960

Milkweed Editions is committed to ecological stewardship. We strive to align our book production practices with this principle, and to reduce the impact of our operations in the environment. We are a member of the Green Press Initiative, a nonprofit coalition of publishers, manufacturers, and authors working to protect the world's endangered forests and conserve natural resources. *The Wish Book* was printed on acid-free 100% postconsumer-waste paper by Friesens Corporation.

For Felix . . .

More powerful than dynamite

THREE

FOUR

The WISH BOOK

What is the grass?

—WALT WHITMAN

Boundless

Let's go my little paradise,
My little heart attack—

The city is unwinding.
Roots are busting through

Concrete. Soon, it will no
Longer be the epoch of racing

In circles. There'll be no more
Sleeping in the Xerox machine.

All those disposable hours
Where we sat around wondering

How many times you could
Tell someone that you loved

Them before they'd explode
Instead of leaning into

Their warmth & actually saying
It. Soon, no one will want unlimited

Texts because it will be known—
This here right now, this,

Exactly what you mean—
Is brought to you by

Every second that happens
Hereafter & how the sunrise

Holds your closed eyes.
Any time is the best time

For us to go. Please, hold my hand.
It is such a pleasure to be

Not dead & walking through
This place with you.

ONE

I Knew You Before You Were

Rusty chains coiled in the cardboard box
    I carry to the dumpster & all I am

Thinking is my face falling off & is yours
    Under it & or is someone's I don't

Even know—further down, a stranger,
    A dead man, a saint, or just a sprawl

Of gravel & then I'm thinking this other thing—
    There's a snake in this box, blacktailed

& then more: there's a bottomless immensity
    Beneath my feet & what a sacrifice

It is each day just to get by, this alchemy,
    This fevered life: illness & love,

Lockjaw & slow-motion kidnappings—it is what
    It always is—chronic dying, shivering with

Unbelievable joy & not knowing a damn thing
    About anything as lightning

Jigsaws the horizon. At the garbage pile, I pause—
    Take a deep breath & sit on the curb.

Like they're being sucked into the sky,
    The trees' limbs lift. No cars on

The street—so quiet. So hushed I can
    Hardly breathe. Thousands of lives

Are piled into all this dirt we walk
    On & I'm waiting, saving it all for you.

After The World Did Not End

I'm a big jellyfish,
All grown-assed—I can

Admit it now: I am
A gelatinous head

Inside of a head
That smells of spit-

Up diamonds that's
Been jammed inside

Another head that,
Most certainly,

In oftentimes slats
Of moonlight, looks

As if a mustache
Has been Sharpied

Above its lip.
So what if the years

Haven't taught me
How to hold

Another's hand,
Tenderly, or drink

Orange smoothies
From the skull

Of my enemies?
My ribs don't cradle

Me right & maybe
I like feeling as if

I'm slipping out
Of the enormous hand

That's puppeting me.
But when the baby

Cries & tears jewel
His cheek's fat

Ledges, I fit into
Myself with the burn

Of a dislocated
Elbow being reset.

Watching him
Sleep today I'm on

Fire. I want to
Rip deep holes

In my body & umbrella
Over him—welcome

His shallow breaths
Into me as he rocks

A clockwise circle,
Eyelids tremoring

With white-hot dreams.

Ghost Rock

O there are so many
Mixed signals in this life—
This way, highway, that
Half, no way, not even

Halfway. The next day
Is all Beep. Bop. Boop.
Can you hear me
Now, motherfucker?

But you & I are both lost,
O so lost. At night, God,
Or some other blowhard,
Whispered in my dreams,

If you love danger you'll die
By it, so I stopped playing tag
With bottle rockets & Roman
Candles. The fourth-story

Window was no longer an option
On the list of things I want
To leap out of before I die.
But I can't help it—I had to

Smash through the sliding
Door & pose like the Heisman
Trophy to show all the people
At my birthday party that glass

& I are pretty much the same
Thing. It's made me think
About it a bit more. Both
Billy Joel & Iron Maiden—
Even that one-armed drummer

From Def Leppard—say only
The good die young, right?
 So, what about being a bit
Of both? Containing more

Than they want me to?
I know, I know, who do I
Think I am? I can hardly
Fathom the one thing I want

To know: when I flatten a hand
Against my sleeping boy's belly
Why do I feel a tiny paradise howling
Through my ribs? The way we fawn over

The untarnished beauty of skin
Is precious & cancerous, I suppose.
What is he, but a pulsing sack
Of wheeze? Help me, please.

Tell me, please. I will beg.
What is this rough magic
That fills me, this blaze
That keeps pushing us on?

Still Life With Birthday Cake & Dynamite

I was alive when this started
But now, well, who knows

What you'd call this pretty
Little place now? Even after all

That E. coli, I've still got one
Leg that kicks. I've never been

To Waco. I've never been
To Baton Rouge. But I've lived

In an apartment where something
The realtor wouldn't speak

About happened. It was amazing,
How life was altered as I sat

In the living room eating a bowl
Of rice, imagining what kind of

Butchery happened—the stained
Hardwood beneath my coffee

Table. Just like today's clouds.
Plumes of acrid smoke are

Wafting above the city & somehow,
I woke with good vibes, thinking

Today was still going to be
A good day. All of the ghosts

Were creep-crawling around
The sugar bowl, right where

I can keep an eye on them.
& that rusty spoon, that bent

Up piece of scrap? Hold the warm
Metal to your lips, my little man.

It's been burning, buried
In my chest for years.

Not Here Not Now

At the very bottom
Of my spirit I have

Bright scissors & a
Deep despair, knowing

The panty-clad gods enjoy
Each our selfish moments—

All the slumber-party-
Handcuffs. The slow dancing

With pillheads. O to smash
Up this endless hallway—

Life's swelling sickness.
This hate mansion filled

With hospital moans.
O to be unsure in any

Flesh. I'm right here
Beside you. Don't cry.

TWO

Pure Missing

Let us be true
To our own
Oblivions, the

Atom bomb
Cradled in
Our mouths.

How the heat
That blooms
When talking

About graves
Collapses the
Room each

Of us carries
Inside. O perfect
Beasts. O raunchy

Goodness. It
Only hurts when
The heart purrs.

Life & Life Only

I stare out the window, dead-
Weighted with the ghosts

Of all the pretty voices
I've known. Waiting: there's

No loneliness more pure.
Just close your eyes & then

Where'd everybody go?
Each moment growing

More & more full. Swaying
Husks of the forever-standing

Sunflowers. Shade giving
Purple to black as the hours

Pass. Echoes of last night's rain
Fingertip over the birdbath's edge.

Sparkling ropes of light, the drops
Dazzle through the nearer dark.

Maybe You'll Be Young & Pretty Forever

Afternoon sunlight
Hammocks through

The rain-laden
Lilacs, beautifully—

But it's no balm.
Daylight carves—humidity

Curdles the air—sharp-
Edging our shapes,

Illumining our despair,
The wretched beasts

Inside us. I know
You're tired, baby,

But it is what it is—
All of our bones

Will quiver & snap. Please:
Tell me that you know

All things will ultimately
End. Please: shout, No, no,

No, everything will last
Forever. Soon, night

Will cloak in with an owl-
Colored darkness webbed

With the dull ember blush
Of sleepless street rovers.

Pearled, languid. How
Lavishly our hurts glow.

Wake Up Dead Man

I got to have whip-
Smart & boom

& no one's
Getting any—

Midnight's jiggling
Light says

Last call
& doomsday

Or everything's
Going straight-

Up live voltage
& it'll all be

Good when I
Wake I promise

Myself, I sing
Baby baby—

The horrible
Roar of this

Ordinary can't
Stop the goody-

Goody-show
How beautiful—

I came to save
The day & now

I'm wondering
How I got here

They'll Be Passing Out Lifejackets Soon

It's so good to finally see
    You shaking

Your moneymaker, lightning-
    Legging through

The gout of these ghost-
    Hours—electric-

Mouthed, chugging cow's blood.
    For you—steam hunkers

Over the leech barrel, the honey-
    Drippers drip.

The pleasure junkies' fever swells
    Our hearts with blood-

Black poison. Hip-shakers, bread
    Makers—everyone is dying

To meet you, baby. They're all pearl-
    Eyed, way up on it & are so

Done talking about it. They're ready
    To go—the best beasts pulling

For the feast—so, if after a minute you
    Still don't know what you want,

Please, don't you worry your sugarmines
    Weak. Just work it, crush

Tonight like a joy-god & hello-hello,
    The candy jar opens. Finger

The glass lip, scabby with pulse-wet
    Grease. Soak it up. Suck it down.

Sink. It's ineffable—the wilding terror,
    The sweet mixture of glow & dark,

A hummingbird caged beneath
    Our ribs. It's good to come

Creeping, ain't it? That black bag over
    The head, that up-in-flames

Feeling. Damn—how long has it been?
    All this illness & the busted-up

Peek-a-boo machine whispering we're all
    Going to die—I might never sleep

Again. This night is everything we might
    Ever have. Every down-the-road,

One day, neverday necking breath
    You'll take is shoe-horned into *right*

Now's stickiness, this moment's many-
    Chambered fragilities. Sting everyone

With kisses, goddamn it—we're still
    Alive! Bother the flesh

Rough & wonderful before the eyes
    Are wax-sealed & unsure.

We can't tell a beginning
    From a hot hot end.

Haruspex

Cricket song helps
The dead become
Comfortable
Being dead.
There are
Baby faces
In the turned-
Up dirt. The
Leeching wear
Of everyone's
Stiff skin.
The crisp air's
Brittle caress.
The wind is
Your favorite
Mixtape melting.
Go with us.
Barrel of sparks,
Boombox dump-
Sters. Come
Now. One more
Step & it's a
Shallow pit
Of red-hot
Coals. Get fresh
With the man
On fire. Get
Close to the
Hotness. How

Icky, the compost
Of burning hair.
The stickiness
In your palm.
Hold on, hold.
You're already
Forgetting how
Far we've come.
Don't say any-
Thing, listen to
Us purr the let
Go, the unfolding.
We're just going
To etch the song
Into you—deep
Down, all of us
Want, at the last
Second, to change
What we've done.

My Favorite Coup d'état

That raging inside me
Shouts *It's time to blow
Kisses, time to sing bye-bye.*

Fingers of sunlight pock
The growing shadows.
The city is darker than black.

The day's almost midnight
& most of the secrets have
Been revealed. Everyone

Dirty-talks to themselves
At night. Everyone is guilty.
Admit nothing when they come

For you. Speak in tongues. Say you
Let Jesus take the wheel—
Whisper *He was just right here.*

Falling Asleep In A Stranger's Bathtub

There ain't nothing
Pleasant in this

Life—a death industry
Of skullduggering

Simpletons & fat
Cat ass-scratchers.

I don't care if you suppose
That all this scar-faced

Prettiness is good for
Someone. *Whoopee!*

Someone's chest is
Getting hairier. Each day

A sunset of painkillers
& at midnight you feel

As if your sleeping cap's
Been nailed to your head

With lightning. Just
Like you, I'm afraid

To close my eyes—
Surer than shit that

If I'm lucky enough to wake
My limbs will all be gone.

Rube Baby Rube

We walked through town like the ghosts
Of dead children throwing apples through

Porch windows—we couldn't decide between
Night clubbing & ice fishing. Either way

We'd be able to kill—you know—killing it
With our dance floor moves or whacking

Carp heads on the ground. I wanted it
All behind me. The synthesizer wind,

The way spoken words felt
Like herpes ulcerating my mouth.

We leapt from the dock onto the frozen
Lake—jumping up & down to make

Sure. I could hear them coughing
Behind me in the dark when I ran

Away. The snowballs they threw landed
In the black like footfalls. I kept on until

There was nothing but cold. I dove
Headfirst & slid—my face a plow.

It filled my insides, glazed my ribs,
Varnishing away thoughts before I'd

Even had them. Before I might laugh
Or even, into the blustery night, bawl.

Pole-Dancing With Ghosts

In one life or another
You will have sex
While a kung-fu movie

Hi-Yas! on a bedroom TV
In front of you. Think of
It: A scrotum accidentally

Karate chopped right off.
Heart cords ecstatically
Torn apart like Twizzlers.

Outside, garbage trucks
Or maybe, the way
These days are going,

A column of tanks.
In another life you fill
Your home's rooms

With old coffee cans
That you don't remember
Stuffing with rusty screws

& nails & rubber bands
& a century of fingernails.
Another life is too goddamn

Hot under the big top—
The bearded lady's stoic
Grace, a dozen plates wobble-

Spinning atop swords. But there
Will be constants: in each life
You'll have 5 million hairs

On each of your bodies,
Just like a gorilla. There will
Always be a never ending

Unfolding inside you & life
After life you'll shed
Hundreds of pounds of skin.

And The Wind Sings Boo

You know you're in
The choicest of spots,
When, staring out the window
You feel a gaping void wheeze
Inside you. Bang, bang, bang,
Flounders a bluebird against
The plate glass. Slap, slap,
Thump, drops the sad truth
Through your bones. So there
It all is. Live Oak. Magnolia.
Mulberry bush. No one
& everything. All there.
Edged sharp by the white-
Hot sun, an old woman wheel-
Chairs by, gnawing at
The mush in her fist
Beneath the tiny umbrella
Duct taped to the chair.
Everyone & nothing.
All of it, of us. Good old
American folk with our
Failing & voluptuous bodies.
Dogs bark as she scoots
By the bluebonnets planted
On the street's edge. I say
Pick a number, any number—
There are millions of ways
All of this is being destroyed
& who, what's next? What

Needs us? I say, I say, I say—
The wheelchair is just a ball
Of silvery light down the street
When I see the car out there
That can parallel park without
The driver. What is that music?
What fills my ears when I watch
My neighbor lift his hands
From the wheel & give me
A thumbs up, grinning
As the sleek-curved car
Reverses perfectly
Into the tight spot?

They Know Not What To Do
With Their Suffering

They're gleeful—accident-prone
Gods or just accidentally gods—

Let's call it hi-def smut.
The dirt is tired from so

Many buryings. We dislike
The lack of flamingoes

In our cities. But the biggest
Challenge is just getting in

To the fun-fun club. It's brutal—
How you see in your reflection

Blisters, lines of fear.
The moths are sharp, violets

Are exploding. It is fine
To call this sublime & be

Wrong. All the waltzing light.
Pearled pigeons in the shadows.

Here are the embalmers
Of figs. You can never go back.

Disneyfication

There were bars on the windows
But until they started with the rope
Games I was allowed to roam out
Onto the balcony that hung
Over a swimming pool that was
Filled from lip to concrete lip
With giant princess heads & real
Live long-eared dogs. The smell
Of chlorine made my eyes water.
It ran my nose. After a few weeks,
My eyes were still blurred & wet
But I tasted smoked oysters & pickles.
The enormous heads bobbed from
End to end. Like knobby planets,
Some spun in place. The bassets,
Churning to stay afloat, bayed.
Who knows where all their shit
Went? Those days were beautiful.
Each day, so there'd still be a bit
Of meat in my hoagie, I fluttered
Two slices of ham shavings down
On the huge-headed characters
When the masked gunmen weren't
Around. It was amazing! The way
A nude woman wearing a deer head
Could do the splits & still catch a parachute
Of lunch meat in her frozen deer mouth.
The unicorn-man speared each one, bullseye,
Then saluted the *MISSION ACCOMPLISHED*

Banner. Often, the *USA Today* was tossed up
To me. I didn't care that they were soaked,
Skunked up & uriney. Like a hamster, I was
Saving a bit of each meal in my cheek until
After bed check & lights out. But soon,
The maggoty pile of edibles in my closet
Began shrinking. I watched the quarter-
Sized flies lift into the air, swiping my
Scraps away. I watched them fly right out.
The sky was blue, always a terrific blue.
I stared endlessly. I fell in love with
The rapturous buzzing in my head.
But this morning, waking from my dream
Of white bulls careening through a factory
Where robots manufactured latex garden
Gnomes on one conveyor belt & sex
Toys on the other, a bad feeling cinched
My bowels. No matter how hard I tried
To blink I could not close my eyes.
They wore bandanas & promised
To use techniques that wouldn't leave
Marks, but a few minutes into it, bruises
Were cauliflowered down my chest & legs.
Blindfolded, they forced me to bob for
Apples in what I soon found out was
A bathtub filled with dead goldfish.
I passed out. I woke up. I passed out.
A gong sounded at some point. I watched
Their shiny boots line up, march in
Place & then trudge out of my room.
A hairless cat sat atop a prosthetic leg
On the mantel & like thrown javelins,

Pool cues stuck from the wall. It felt
Like a vibrating halo had been screwed
Into my head. I looked in the mirror
& saw a double-decker toy racetrack
Had been drilled into my skull. Two
Cars raced 'round & 'round. My hair
Was flat on one side. The cars would
Not stop. Stork bites covered my face
& from the looks of it, I'd never have
An erection again. There was a rumbling
Downstairs—I felt it in my toe bones.
Cigarettes were being smoked outside.
They'd been on my wrists so long, going
Without handcuffs seemed unnatural. Above
My chin, I felt the beginning of words
But only heard a wet, mashing sound
Like a driveway of too-ripe peaches
Being rolled over by a Buick. Above
My chest, I felt nothing. Outside, the sky
Went milky dark & the speakers started
Blasting Barney, then baby screams.
I looked in the mirror—what had happened
To me? Where did I make the wrong
Turn? The man in the mirror shamed
Me with his finger, then held it to his lips.
The little cars circled & vroomed, dizzying
Me. With the squirrel head I had repeatedly
Refused to wear in my lap, I sat on
The bed's edge. The furred mask's toothy
Smile curved up at me like a waning moon.
Never never, I gurgled to the ecstatically blank
Eyes, but I saw my reflection & shuddered.
The pitter-patter in my chest felt heavier than ever.

The Blowdown

It's hard to imagine a day
When I'm not scratching
My nuts right at God.

Everyone I love shuffles
Toward the sun & I am
Measuring my chewed

Off fingernails into this
Here bucket. Always a bit
More. Always too much.

So supersonic goes a blur
In the sky & the sweet peas
Shudder. So I'm head to

Head with all of today's
Ghosts. I stare from
The shadows when the dragsters

Burn by. Rims gleaming like spit
Dangling from the baby's mouth.
I know you dream of saving me,

As if I were some kind of Chilean
Miner. But my genome is half skink
& I mostly foam at the mouth.

I might say get me out of this hole
But what I mean is I don't want to be
Trapped up there with all of you.

Watch—each time I put
My foot down, my arms
Rise into the air. Land

That jet. Score that touchdown.
I've been told hundreds of times
That I'm a really good hider

When I'm wearing your clothes—
Short black skirt, the pillbox
Hat. But the word on the street

Is that I taste like intensive
Care. So now, I'm preparing
For the deep sleep by snorting

Pepper flakes & slapping
My chest like an Olympic
Swimmer. In whatever time

I have left, I'm going to be
The best disaster I can be.
Crunches. Pull-ups. Protein

Bars. Arms outstretched,
I'm sprinting at you
Like the Hindenburg.

Marooning

So often
We are
Missing

Out on it—
Ill-equipped
To imagine

The day any
Different than
We hoped it

Might be,
The forth-
Springing world

Unzippering
Our chests
To the insight

Of midnight
Cowling over
The front yard

& a stranger
Down-heading-
It through sheets

Of rain, back & forth

With dead chickens
Drooped in his hands.

Where lightning bursts
Translate back into
A timorous & glottal

Language, quaking
Lusters that lace
The dark sky, in

& out & ever almost,
As all of it vanishes
Before our eyes

This Pledge Drive Don't End

I know what you're thinking—
There's a whole lot of negative

Energy in this room & it's starting
To remind you of the terrible

Months you spent as an infant.
All rashed-out thinking those

Crazy baby thoughts about how
All the big people seem so small-

Minded, leaving you on the roof
During the noonday sun, where

You stared into that brilliant orb
For hours & later told yourself,

So you wouldn't suddenly break
Down, that love is love no matter

How many words accidently
Slip out & slap you. So, the air

Smells of last night's screams.
What are we gonna do about it?

Our neck of the woods is just
Block after block of phantom limbs

Anymore—when the cops bust in
It's impossible to kick your feces

At them. It's not worth worrying
About it. Get back in line, we all have

To get our scarlet letter sooner
Or later. It's a fact, jack—everyone,

You, me, Gandhi & the Hamburglar,
We're all someone's baby-powdered bitch.

Volant

Alive in the ghost
Park, I am this

Darkness. The horizon
Is a boil of halved

Strawberries shining
& illness stitches me

To the glittery
Dirt. My hands are

Broken. They are
Electric with the raw

& bleeding organs
Of beloved pets.

This world is cruel
To all things but its

Grace is unimaginable.
The unraveling light

Writes messages as
Shadows stretch

From sugar shack
To whisper-winded

Playground. *Are you*
Almost finished licking

My wounds clean?
In the empty

Swimming pool,
One flip-flop,

A disposable
Razor. A rider-less

Skateboard hums
Back & forth. Spider-

Cracked concrete.
Spider-cracked skin.

Last night, I could
Have sworn

That cherry-red
Coronas bloomed

In the sky. I ate
Without knowing

What crunched, what
Metallic sweetness

Burst & filled
My mouth. This

Morning when
I opened my lips

To murmur *I love
You* to the yolky

Daylight, horse
Flies buzzed out

Of my throat.
Marrowsong,

Dreamwonder—
Tell me, trumpet

It through the city's
Steel & cinderblock

Valleys, please,
Let me feel it—

What broken
Animals, what

Beasts make it
To the other side?

7-7-7

Each morning after
I slip into the rabbit-
Skin mask & make
A *whoop-whoop* call
To the beyond
I stare, unblinking,
At my belly—practicing
The urge to give birth
To myself as each
Breath the hot coal's
Steam syrups my
Insides & the scorched
Yard looks just about
Ready to become
A hammock between
The two worlds.
It's the Texas sunrise—
The sunlight's certain
Slant that makes fire
Appear to be emerging
From each house
Window, but already,
I know the world
Of the dead—flames
Lick out from my feet
When I hopscotch
Through the cemetery,
Stumbling through
That last step a bit—

So still, that dog appears
Every couple of days
With an apparition
Of black butterflies
Flurrying from its jaw—
I guess it's still those little
Things that get me
Sometimes—chewing
A #4 pencil or glancing
Out the sink window
As I scrub a pot & BOOM—
There I am again—tip-
Toeing that doomy edge—
The room aspirin-white,
Chunked pieces of my heart
Puddling on the table
As I try to shape it
Into something workable.
So I'm slot machine, a black
Box whispering from
The bottom of the sea.
I've come so far. I'm so close.

Not Yet A Word, Climbing Out Of Your Little Cage

It is pre-love & guttural, midnights
Of peeping into strangers'

Windows, hoping to see
That sometimes, everything

Can be right. Aborted lullaby
& tepid tongue—the wind coming

Up, the wind homewarding
Through the hopscotched streets.

Little outward, little sputum—
From clasp, where night

Is a spider-crack of falling
Pecans, to the choke hold

Of what can be seen. All of it
Decided, then. All of this

Seeable—it all already happened
Sometime before fire became fire.

So encore. So one last time. So rust-
Weakened hinges singing *pretty, pretty, poof.*

THREE

Real-Live Bleeding

If you can bring nothing to this place
but your carcass, keep out.
                    —William Carlos Williams

Step right up my little fearfuls
    Bellow blue in this pornography

            Heaven—it's true for the whole
            Stinking family—downright

    Amazing & a hundred percent always
    Yes yes yes!

            Just five bucks & O my—
            Welcome the razzle dazzle—
                    Parades, bobbing balloons

You'll cry watching the alligator
    Man drink from the open hydrants' gush

Gaze at punk faces in the wet-grooved
    Shapes of freshly skinned knees

        Ammonia fumes! Cloud Swings!
        It's up to you—come in
            Come in!

Sit in the star backs & watch
    The impossible hippodrome!
            Test us! Break our iron jaws

Like it's the bottom of the ocean
The arcade's filled with salty light

So it's time to kiss
My blackberry
Lipped bastards

For baby needs milk & pink lasting neon

Everyone in line smells
The liverdug worming
Beneath your ribs

Under these backlit skies
Croons of hallelu from the shooting
Gallery's ribboned red stars

Trebles of birds plushed above
In the thresholding dark—

There is a grappling at the freak show door—
Everything—hair-
Line-cracked

Just for the hipped-glow
Glimpse
Of pretty pretty girls

Winking strands of light drape finely
Over the midway's pearled boxes

Where big old cake eaters press
To their faces with hot love—

The butcher's pretzels, the butcher's lemonade
    All the butcher's edibles—

Blood-tipped embers walk
    The back end's fringed dark

& still no one believes that coralline moon
    Is just a thin knot pooled & waiting
        To hang the heart

On this carousel the horses' ivories flash, bursting
    Eyes vein & gleam so all of your secrets

  Are safe & rounding: your head
  Chopped off each time you wake

  Slivered apart in your sleep for all
  The pearldust caking the insides

  Of your head   Murderfilled splotches
      Of mouths cushioned with taffy as you

  Roam & round again on the poled colts
     Lightstrung, the music trembly

    Mouths of the shriekers webbed
        With sword-swallowing song

Close your eyes my sweet volunteer: imagine yourself
    Split open like a gunnysack—

You're red-oiled & they strut
    Like peacocks around your shred-bone city

Those great festively holed fellows humming
    Your future & you understand perfectly

Well that I know the jack of spades is what
    You're thinking by how your lip quickens

    Which means I also know that one wish
        You have each inflatable day

So sad, how you want so very little—

    Socketed with the comfort
    Of this carnival screaming

    Such glorious chumps when you listen
        With your eyes closed

        As unwieldy & dangle-faced

            They hang

Believe if you must the sun endlessly
    Rising & falling over the big cats—

    It is a remarkable tangle
        In this life beholden

To slick-pitted weather & feverish sugars

    You: swollen with this illness
      Called being alive—

      Those diced apples
      Carmeled & circled
      Around the paper plate

As you finger the picnic table & count
        Listening kindly
           Listening lost

For swaddled in night's ink
    What is meant by any fear

Is color: flush
    To suffer impossibly

Narrow skulled glow-in-the-dark tattoos
    & bleached & duct taped coffins

Elephant ears pocketed silent
    In sleepless cheeks

You want to look
    In the show mirror & see
        A different slough

        Fingers blistered—
            Spikelet & stickily
            Praising

A convent in the black-limbed copse—
    The swill in stair-stepping hips

The human pincushion's
    Hot-watered eyes

Against your deafness the barkers repeat
    Everyone's winding longing
        They repeat over & over

    The longing switchblade
Of grasses tilting with light

Up in slivers
    From the cook house's concrete

O how much you love the dark ride

    The diggers' claws
        Everchaining

In a house of mirrors it is your body
    Tethered to nothing

Of this earth   the exquisite silken
    Light where little dramas

Are found in corners of ratted
    Trash & spilled drinks—

So clean up & come over
    See how she fits
        In this there box

For just a quarter you know
    She couldn't do it

With any clothes we'll see if you
    Can hold your beautiful

Breath until all the awnings drop

Dare to trust each nut & bolt you gather
    From the sand-fisted dark

After watching them fling
    From the Tilt-a-Whirl rocking on

    Beneath the branches
Put them under your tongue

For night comes to bear your
              Gasps here

    Share in the wayward dark
        Your dripping candies
            & the four horned
Goat is free—

    Two-headed cows & call it
    Love when the trains racket by

The meat-sawed just between flashing
       & nobody but you can taste

That part inside you roaming
       Untrue & crossroaded lovely

Gravel from the steel wheels pinging—
    Rumored pelts of your
          Savor-lobbing life

Because all the crocus bushes praise dumpster fires
    & their cinder-blown pity

    Human dynamo: you must
        Have a good time
    In the lastly upward night

Where they swing—
    Chant & mock the bones

Now & again neon against a porcelain sky
            For it is always sunup

    & you are plagued—
            Sharp-toothed staring into the barest
            Of swirling branches

Fast-counting men with perfect hair
        Under the moonlight
   Dressed in white yellowed

Posters of beloveds pocking the lampposts
     & in the shadows
        The careful French kissers

But somewhere out in the dark—
           The slaughter of pigs

That suffering & cloven
   Dislocation of mistrusting beasts

With no harsh agitation of day in the sky

   You are getting closer
The strong-armed sun does not
   Even half-want to shine

With midnight clouds ruffled above
    Suddenly your head

Is vivid with fireworks booming
The unstoppable rushing of stars—

    Next door or haunted: they are
    Ready-made in the walking cemetery

    The limply whistling heat
        Of half & half body parts

Cherry-faced & straining
   In the straitjacket

More willing with smiles down there
   In the mining dark for a dollar

To unhinge a bone from a shoulder socket
   To against press   To be torn

———◆———

Who could fail to believe all this
   Being born on summer nights
          Pink-faced & grim

Under the fast counting light gliding
Over the one they will find considerably
Purple & smash-nosed in the morning park

But it is always so fascinating
   The baby wrapped
         In trash beneath July stars

For this here is the fireball show
    A foolish of brightness in the turning
        City of us cripples

Hoarse rivulets of grave light
    Glowing the winners' bagged goldfish

As all of the creaking things going away
    & the bodybox scrapes

Its way through the gates
    Into the pleasure garden

You lisp & words fall swampy—

        Pink-lipped into a rusted bucket
        Thin with peanut shells & spit

        Clanging away around the gourd
        Of your sheet-metalled insides

Where a boy with a plastic bag over his head
Pretends to pick fruit from the dead apple tree
        Of your heart

Grease from eyelid to toenail
   In the roller derby

      You better believe it

      The horrible filigree of your face
Against beamrots never erasing

& how outside & above: the lightning baskets
   The sky, thunder crowing your eyes

As you listen to the bull's-eye of your body
   Preach & palsy the rain beads

For night always tears windstruck
   & you are still always this
      Big deal of dying

Watching the scurry to snap & lock down
   The tarps & settle
      The lowing animals in tents

   While you sing into your pruning hands

O glass benders & grind
    Here it is!   The wheel of fortune

Flattened with glitter & last call
At the wax museum—your face, your face!

        Floss, I promise floss!

An end all syrupy & perfect

So come on   come on

     There's no reason not to
       & not a bit of time left

No one believed
    You'd come back anyway

    So if it makes you feel any
    Better we'll call you lucky:
                Constellated with darts

But go ahead & sit there in the rivering dirt
    As lights flash above you if you must

    Your insides
           Can't stop caterwauling

Next time around we'll name you healed!
    Body in a fishbowl!
        Body in a bag!

You little man unloosed
    Amongst the shufflers & sick

FOUR

The Pleasure Dome

If nothing lasts forever—not the stars
    In the black above

Or your hollow-chested look—what's
    With all this misery?

How many times do we have to be told how
    It goes? Our dreams will come

True & life will be Beyoncé's thighs & *The Ballad*
    Of Ira Hayes & hot tub limos

& cinderblock-sized turkey legs.
    & then, when you're not looking

They'll start drilling gramma's tomb
    For oil & flames will blossom

From the faucet & just when you're
    Starting to feel it, the party

Will start winding down. You'll find
    Yourself out front, smoking

In the cold. Tilted cups spilling as you stare
    Up at the sky's brilliant streaks.

Steam will rise from the burrows in the front-
    Yard snow. From the holes

In your busted-up face.

It will be last call. It will be the most
    Perfect midnight of your life.

Right then, when it all seems like gravy,
    Your dreams will shatter

& turn on you. They'll choke you out
    & stuff you into the trunk

Of a late model Ford no one will tell
    The police they remember

Seeing screech off into the foreclosing dark.
    From then on, each day

You'll wake utterly lost. The infinite
    Voodoo of your jean pockets

Filled with shit—each morning,
    Without fail, more shit!

But what do you do? It's the price
    Of doing business, right?

We're the primo supreme, the luckiest
    Of the dumb! Still almost

Running in a straight line—flapping
    Our wicked mouths!

We had our good run, our fevered
    Dreams & joyous sweating.

Besides, nobody wants to slather
    The excrement on like war

Paint & paint the town brown. To bark
    At the feral moon. Until

Someone Valsavas with everything they
    Have to sing, I say fuck

The dumb! Supersize my barely beating heart
    & tell me again that this, right here,

Is as good as it gets—We dance all night
    With beautiful corpses draped

Over our shoulders. Bombs star-
    Bursting when we breathe.

Your Life Is The Bed I'm Gonna Lie Down In

Nothing is quite the savor
That was promised. No salvage
In the rough & tumble but still
The darksome bellows down
Below songs: Heartbreaker.
Consuming the tragedies. Clang
Smut. Lately, I'm feeling
Too much—so let me give
You a sliver of the ecstatic.
The emptying darkness cracks
Open. I'm terrible with names
But I want the whole grist
Mill to pile on. This body wants
To break out of itself. Listen
To the dirt mattress gossip
Its buryings. Tentatively,
I'm long dead. Come sunup
Everyone will taste brutal,
Become a vessel of waltzing
Light. The moral of this
Proposition is to find a way
To leave them crying. I have
Fifteen dollars—I'd love to hear
You speak through that mask.
Tell them that everything is
Wonderful, but you won't be
Back for a long time. The fun
Cage is open for business, always.

We're going to call whatever
Happens *Deer Hunting & Fantastic*
Go Ahead for the narrowing vision
After the tendering. You'll be all
Light, turned inside out & never
Going back. You'll be glowing no
Sleep the whole paradise tomb.

Of Love Hot & Enormous

Render me undone & little lumps first—
For what impossible solace

You've made of my fear, my freedom.
All sweet & gone like. Remind me again

How fun it is to be licked fever-stricken,
Wearing a rabbit skull necklace & shouting

Emergency. I miss the beginning, opening
Was so tender & monstrous. There was

A bringing hunger that caused trapdoors
To open all across the body. They told,

Whispered our stories & lists—sun-rippled
& grab-fucking & troglodytes with gold-

Rimmed nostrils huffing paint, leaving
A trail of spit right up to this here

Now. In these parts, it seems a person,
To feel like a real live, electric-blooded

Person, is urged to seek with rolled-back
Eyes, swallow as much as possible. This

To be the person fatbacking the days,
The one aglitter with graves.

The sky's rising traceries sing *everything*
Is wonderful, everything is marvelous.

But straight-up, we are an oblivion
Of wants—the baby will only eat giraffe-

Shaped crackers, the giraffe isn't part
Leopard or camel but the trio are

All bush-meat & I double take at
The postman's cheek-growth

Because it's gotten even bigger
& strange gurgles seem to sprout

From it. What to call this beautiful shame
Crawed in the throat of us animals?

I promised myself to the highest
Bidder. I promised myself fragile

& perfect & then ignored my falling
Apart. But who's the lucky

Homunculus? So often, everyone forgets—
We're a parade of illness. Many of us

Will wander out the front door & never
Be found. Our fingertips go mealy & today,

Blow out the candles little princess—the kid
On the milk carton would be celebrating

His fifty-fifth birthday. We're all no-gravity
& floating sunward in the end. I feel it

Like a sauna behind my eyes—nothing

Is more important than jubilation
& grind. So rather than *this*—I can be

Ready at a moment's notice. I've prepped,
Tangle-plushed & coming in this

Bootleg divine. My heart swells bigger,
Stronger. It's promised to explode.

Shakedown Machine

Do you smell that? Here, where everything looks
Perfect? That sour tang of a pile of one hundred degree
Garbage behind the storefront you're standing in
Front of. Sniff the air. Look around. But hurry,
You have a whole life of Miss Pancake Face
Pageants & unicorn shows to go to. The window shine
Is all you can see—the shine makes all the puppet
Strings invisible. Everything is great, man. Everything
Is groovy. Beast Sounds! Beach Loving! Everyone knows
That this is the best island filled with the most beautiful
People. Stand tall, sneer. Karate chop evil, & then blow
Kisses. Deny any & all acts of indecency, the degeneracy
Of a hotel room filled with motorboat-engined phalluses—
All that gravy—the pleasure cruises & sex boats.
Even a noseless victim of the Butt Naked Brigade
Would say something stinks. Right here in River City.
In Cowtown. In the city of lights, of sighs, of plum-
Picking & Juggalos. This buttery burg. This village
Of apple-bottomed veejays. Take a big old whiff.
Take it & wait. Maybe you'll shrug, because maybe
It really doesn't matter. What's the difference
Between gulag & goulash, anyway? But perhaps
That last lungful will make you shudder, ask yourself
What's the matter, you burning? & maybe, just maybe,
You'll remember that fable your mother often told you—
A world populated by fisty gimps & sex slaves & people
Who call, say they do what they do because they're doing
It for you, all those monsters that smile their hate. A land
Where no one repents. A land where no one should be

Unrepentant. A land where, each dusk you hear faint
Voices, a choir, softly in the udder-colored haze,
Harmonizing, devotedly singing, *bring out the wackos*.

Listen Now Pull It Together Focus

If you want to survive this
Downturn, sooner or later
You're gonna have to dedicate
Yourself to hunger-related
Crimes & a flickering moral
Certitude. Start ingesting Barry
White-sized doses of HGH.
Hand-eye coordination is
Key: hone it with wiffleball bats
& stink-eyeing strangers.
Stare like you think, when
Grilled just right, they'd taste
About as good as a McRib.
Along with the apocalypse,
Try not to think of the
Meltdown as a series of fuck-ups
That will hurt you, but not,
In any way, the person who
Fucked up & who will, sooner
Or later, fuck up in the exact
Same way. You must think of it
All as a terrible joke whispered
Into the ear of a woman who has
Spent two years in a coma & now,
Once a month, sees her husband
Fondling his new wife when they
Stop by the hospital. Sound bad?
She's alive, right? It's not going
To be easy & it'll be about

As much fun as that game you
Played after getting too drunk
In college—back & forth, you
& your best friend Stash
Kicked each other in the nuts
As hard as you could. These
Are tough times, but don't give up!
Onward! Upward! Everywhere!
Say it loudly: intestinal fortitude!
Say it again, or at least something
Close: fortuitous, flapper hat,
Intestinal parasites & floor-by-floor
Eviction! Come on, grasshopper—
You are better than this Affluenza.
You are better than a Kleenex.
You are better than a gold-plated
Outhouse. The quaintest Midwestern
Towns, all the boarded-up burgs
& close-out final-sale closed-down
Main Streets, are waiting for their king.

Wearing A Dead Man's Sunglasses
To The Zoo

At noon, the moon
Appears out of no-
Where, a ghosty
Plate in the
Scorching blue
Above. Passersby
Smile, sparks bursting
Haloes around
Their ears. It just
Happens sometimes—
You want something
So awfully bad
That bulls careen
Up & down
Your body.
A running in
Your blood & no
Shelter from
The downpour
Of frogs.
Standing in line
To see the Komodo
Dragon is about finding
The right balance
Of dark matter.
Hands shuffling
Through pockets.
Palms tapping

Thighs. The sad grin
Of the woman
Who feels herself
Burning even though
She's not going to
Light herself on
Fire until she sees
The flamingoes.
There's a shifting
Tide inside me
That has
No bottom.

The Itching Is Chronic

Losing a little heart
Is a million times better
Than being chained up

In the backyard. No one wants
To see a Texas sweetheart
Reduced to a sunburnt skeleton,

Especially when fixing that
Blood-pumper is so easy—
A science lab of stem-cell-

Stuffed petri dishes, centrifuging
Rat lungs & Bunsen burners
Fingering with flames.

A month later & you're good as new,
Mr. Potato Head. Heart all white
Lightning. Heart anything you want

It to be. But losing face—
No way, hombre—that's a different
Animal all together. I'd rather

Have Job Syndrome than square
Dance with that disfigured devil.
Tycho Brahe wore a gold & silver

Nose after losing part of his beak
In a duel & what good did
That do him? A debunked planetary

System & death because he
Wouldn't get up to piss
At a party. I don't need

That kind of help. Look: I can
Say the solar system is a fabric
Of hot dogs somersaulting

Through gaseous expansions
& make you think about it
For a second. There are too

Many truths to see in
A half-whole body that won't
Stop moving. Let the record

Show I've cloned a human
In the upper right drawer
Of my desk. It will someday

Be known that atoms are
Infinitesimally small hummingbirds
& whistles are ghosts trying

To tell us what is impossible
To believe about ourselves.
Can you feel it swelling? All noses

Are collapsed goldmines!
The universe is whirling
With the most joyous riblets!

Show Up Look Good

We feed ourselves to the fire
One inch at a time to prove it—

Everything here is a gift we can't
Figure out how to open. No one

Will admit it, but we all want
To rock it rug-burned & neon.

None of us would believe what
We can do. Right this very

Moment, all of us are a mouthful
Closer to swine flu. It might sound

Like a tasty way to go out
But when you wake

From the fever dream, you'll be
Sleeping in the fetal position

In a Dumpster. Fishnet stockings
Wrapped around you, but each

Is filled with hundreds of dead birds.
Think twice: ghosts are always

Tumbling over the bone fort but it's
Got to be happy hour somewhere.

Locked & Loaded

The most amazing
Things happen

In big & empty
Places. The Internet.

Detroit. Soybean
Fields razed after

The harvest. The
Parking lot where

You were tased.
Step back & stop

Yelling questions
At the sky. I'm

Prepared for
The hot hand

Of the inevitable.
My body is scrubbed.

My mouth is minty
Fresh. I'm almost

Ready. Givey, give
The magic words.

Everybody Has A Skeleton

Spinning, we closed our glitter-painted eyes
& sung the alphabet until it no longer felt
Like someone was renting space out in our heads.

We felt on fire, molten, & passed out public service
Announcements about the bone-strengthening
Benefits of hip tosses & heavy metal. We jumped

Until our jawbones went rubbery & our devil-shaped
Hands glistened with spit. Everyone, in perfect
Unison, yelled, *You dog. You silly dog, you,* over & over

& over. It was exhausting. People heaped, heard
Smooth jazz or a jibber-jabber Jesus in their molars.
I ran out of oxygen & remembered the sodden days

Of my youth—what a fool I'd been, believing
That *The struggle to the heights is enough to fill
A man's heart.* & what a sucker I still was, trusting

That day's moonman mathematics. But staring
Up into the clouds, I knew what was next. I hate
To admit it, but I did. I knew, right then, about

The coming hocus-pocus. But like everyone
Else, I just stared around dumbly. There we
Were: A football field filled, sideline to sideline

With La-Z-Boys & bathtubs. I didn't point out
The darkening clouds. Everyone is afraid already.
An old man looked up at me from his chair

& there I was, looking into my own face.
Tucking a blanket around my wet thighs.
Centering my nice little shawl. Lightning

Egg-cracked the horizon again & suddenly, I thought
Maybe it *had* been right all along—it was *struggling*
& the *heights* but I'd been imagining a teeny,

Ill-shaped heart inside me, when a
Humongously bloody & engorged lovemonster
Had been suckling inside me all this time.

The air made my lungs pucker. The bonfire smoke
Made me weep. I poured a bit out, then poured out
A bit more, before shaking the last trickle down

My throat. The old man, the old me & a sky darkening
With facts: even the best among us is not innocent
& without good bones, we could not stand up at all.

Making It Nice

Because the newsman said the end
Was coming soon, we dropped our paper
Plates, ran into the street & praised
Our hands up high after whipping off
Our tear-away pants. We whooped,
Took it all off. It was that kind
Of summer. A new emergency
Every day & today, a heart-attack
Kind of backyard shindig. No matter
What hateful things the haters next door
Yelled, we crowded back into the yard
& hunched around the smoke pit
Like hiding-in-the-bushes masturbators.
Everyone said it was a shame that
We'd never be able to do this again
Because this smelled exactly like
The good old days. Shuttlecocks turned
Into nostalgia in the sky, flying so high
There seemed to be time to think
About everything we wouldn't have
Time to lose. When the wind changed,
From the top of the fence someone pointed
To the rolling plumes on the horizon,
Another said it looked like it was time
For the party to end after all. There
Was a long applause, wolf calls
Even, for the glitter-cheeked woman
Who danced like she'd been possessed
By a jackhammer. After all the false

Starts, this seemed like the real deal.
All the fly-assed party people strolled away
Butt-naked. They waved. I waved back.
It got so quiet. I heard a Chilean pipe band
Coming from somewhere beneath
My ribs. Clothes piles, like Technicolor
Burial mounds, were everywhere.
Something felt sacred about it & I was
Terrified of touching them. I closed
My eyes, stilling my body until
I was beyond numb, until I felt
Dead & I was afraid of nothing.
Like this, I waited & waited. But nothing
Happened. Hours passed. Very little had
Changed when I looked around. I sighed.
The tiny hot dogs that had been bobbing
In BBQ sauce all day were eyeing
Me so I started eating. I wasn't even
Hungry, but I couldn't stop hiding
Them in my mouth. I did the math
In my head: cut in half, add a Crocodile
Mile & a bellyful of ostrich burgers.
I ran the numbers over & over
& each time I was the remainder.
Same old me. It felt like the appropriate
Time for a toast, so I plinked my finger
Against all the abandoned & sweating
Cups around me. When there were no
More to tick, I flicked the air.
Faster & faster—until it sounded
Like footsteps, running. I remembered
The fast dog the neighbors had in my youth.

I'd shout *Look at that dog!* each time
I saw it, even when I was alone. I said it
So much it became a tic. I screamed it while
Making diving catches during softball
Games, just as the lights blinked off
In movie theaters. I said it each time
Someone bit my ear or put a hand
Down the front of my jeans. Above me
The roiling clouds were still roiling.
Moments earlier, I thought I'd seen
My life going down the drain in them
But now I looked a little closer & it wasn't
Mine at all. It was the life of the girl
Who danced so freakily. I'm not sure
Where the tears came from, but they
Sprinted down my face & leapt
From my cheeks with little *Huzzahs!*
Tiny lakes formed around me.
Look at that dog! I whispered
To the puddles, the burst blood
Vessels in the eyes of my
Reflection, *Look at that dog!*

Trust Me Trust Me Trust

When you throw a hand-
Ful of lawn darts into the air

Because a voice in your head
Tells you to—shout *Heads-up!*,

Watch everyone at the BBQ
Geegaw skyward, & then after

Cleaning up the mess, start collecting
Bottled water, SPAM. From then on,

Nothing in your life will ever be
Dire, but, sorry to break it to you,

The end is coming soon. So, drive
With no hands, charge into oncoming

Traffic. Eat those eggs that were best
By sometime last year. You are

One of the chosen—don't think
Too much about what's happening

Around you. Listen to me, now—
Let me in. There's a tremendous

Amount of untapped energy
In staring straight ahead. Hold on

To that. Be positive. A very famous
Person once said that anyone

Can quit smoking but it takes
A real man to face cancer. Buy

Truck nuts & attach them
To your belt. The last days

Will be vivid—practice
For the end by wrapping, again

& again, the cat in Saran Wrap.
Booby-trap the yard with spike-

Sharpened wooden spoons. Sit
Like a pretty little lotus, reading

Survival manuals. It doesn't
Matter if it's in the basement

Or you're spear-fishing at the
Bottom of the pool—you'll no

Longer hear the naysayers
& their ugly living. Don't waste

One tear on all those meatsacks
You called friends. You're only

About the good shit now—
Bring on that everloving jelly.

Ain't No Best In Show

The good time is
A hush-blush show
On these rainy days—

A reverberating bird-
Cage. The live oaks wet-

Sigh over the flophouse
Ground. Delight is
Uncatchable as a rabbit—

Pink feet ripping off each
Time you touch. When I

Was very young every
Night arrived hard-
Coated, a sweet candy.

Now the darkness tells me
It has been my lovely

For a long, long while.
Hello shadows, hello shivery
Black. I swine-leap into

Myself. So much gibberish
Out there in the world, everyone

Two parts not looking

So good & wanting always
To karate-chop someone

Right in the face. The air
Stinks of burning glue.

Only the dug-up tongues
Of dead house pets sing
Truth through the storm.

Lampreys Of Sunlight

The aftermath of a brilliant
Downpour—a shredded oak,

The street tumbling with shingles—
Is nothing compared to the almost

Good feeling a terrific beating
Can give you: how the nearness

Of death strips man unadorned.
But most often, our gift is

The burden of ignorance
& dreams: Sourdough & pickles

At the graveyard picnic &
Each night the woman who

Stands in your kitchen
In nothing but blinding white

Panties combs her lustrous hair
With a four-inch nail. This morning,

I nibbled a two-day old pancake
& realized that, along

The way, everything inside us
Gets broken. The cardinals

Are playing peek-a-boo. Ground-
Ward, the magnolia bends.

Let Us Get Our Gifting On

Like a vulture, I piss
Down my leg so I don't
Overheat. My eyes are

Bloodshot, glassy.
I'm dazed by the list
Of my maladies, slack-

Jawed at all the side-
Show horrors. But I don't
Want to be anyone else

In this, or any other, life.
All around me, there's too
Much to love. That there

Overwatered & now dying
Azalea. The spit-clean
Brick I found balancing on

One of the oak's low branches
Out front. The rubber band
In my pocket. The condom

In the dirt. There was a time
I used to think that a thing was
Created when I saw it, but

It only seems to be ours
When we open our eyes.
Somewhere else, this freak

Show has forever been beautiful.
An envelope of baby teeth.
Wire-framed glasses shoplifted

From an estate sale. Southbound
Birds, that swath of commas
In the sky over Last Truck Lake.

I couldn't sleep last night & at sun-
Up, watched a golden smog slowly
Lacquer the horizon—Another

Morning & I want to save
Everyone. Another morning that
Makes it hard to believe the body
Can hold so much blood.

The Trick Bag

I bury my head in
It & everything tastes

Electric. The sky sings
Jigsawed. Cotton candy

Fills the hollows behind
My eyes. There's a thunder-

Burst in my gut. A crowd
Circles me, snickering.

One crows, *What's up
Mister Monster?* Another

Calls me *Baghead*.
The oilcloth does not

Fit perfectly, but these
Hard times have proven

I can get used
To almost any shade

Of doom. My elastic socks
Droop-sag. Inhaling

The perfect dark, I am just
Born. Inhaling the perfect

Dark, I'm slumber. Inhaling,
I'm so old I might never again see

Tomorrow. Inhaling, I am
Moonshine. Inhaling, I inhale.

On the other side of the eye-
Holes, the day unravels. The

Taunters bully & rage. Ropes
Of light slip through

The swaying grass.
The ground quakes,

A pleasure that climbs me
Settles in my chest.

Whirling, my insides tilt.
I am a ramshackle palace.

The brightness, the din,
Like a car crash. Around me,

It's beautiful stuff—the little
Oblivions smearing as I go.

We will be stardust.

—C.D. Wright

The Wish Book

The moon croons ghost
    & curtains lift

    Into the room magic & shine
      The moon sings

Light of pinball machines
    Over the skin
      Of the world

    The moon whispers pretty pretty
      Pleads for you

The moon croons lost & stare
      A hole in it stare
        It whole

    Love-dusted new each
      Opening time each

      Moth-thin page
        Each dark glowing flesh

Pity those that die the moon sings
    The moon whispers

      Without dynamite the moon
      Pleads the bathtub filled the moon

Bellows bubble-slick
Bawls glory glory
With blood

The moon croons let me
Cover you the moon sings who
Is inside you the moon whispers

Did you hear
Something out there out

There what will you say to them
When I'm gone?

Acknowledgments

Many thanks to the editors of the journals where these poems first appeared, sometimes in other shapes and sizes.

American Poetry Review
Trust Me Trust Me Trust," "Making It Nice,"
"Still Life With Birthday Cake & Dynamite,"
"Wake Up Dead Man," and "The Wish Book"

Bellevue Literary Review
"Pole-Dancing With Ghosts"

Esquire
"My Favorite Coup d'état"

Fifth Wednesday Journal
"Not Here Not Now" and "Rube Baby Rube"

The Florida Review
"Ghost Rock" and "Ain't No Best In Show"

Forklift, Ohio
"This Pledge Drive Don't End"

Gulf Coast
"Of Love Hot & Enormous"

The Kenyon Review
"Your Life Is The Bed I'm Gonna Lay Down In" and
"Maybe You'll Be Young & Pretty Forever"

The Literary Review
"Shakedown Machine"

Los Angeles Review
"The Itching Is Chronic" and "The Pleasure Dome"

The Missouri Review
"I Knew You Before You Were"

Poetry International
"Boundless"

Precipitate
"Lampreys Of Sunlight"

Redivider
"Life & Life Only," and "Locked & Loaded"

Revolver
"The Blowdown," "Marooning," and "Pure Missing"

Salt Hill
"Let Us Get Our Gifting On" and "Show Up Look Good"

Seattle Review
"Real-Live Bleeding"

Smartish Pace
"They'll Be Passing Out Lifejackets Soon"

Sycamore Review
"7-7-7"

Tin House
"After the World Did Not End," "Not Yet A Word,
Climbing Out Of Your Little Cage," and "The Trick Bag"

TriQuarterly
"Disneyfication" and "Falling Asleep In A
Stranger's Bathtub"

Whole Beast Rag
"Haruspex" and "Volant"

Yemassee
"Wearing A Dead Man's Sunglasses To The Zoo"

"Boundless" "and "Shakedown Machine" were
nominated for the Pushcart Prize.

"Not Yet A Word, Climbing Out Of Your Little Cage" is
a line written by Nick Flynn. The poem that appears
under that title was my contribution to an exquisite
corpse that Mary Jo Bang, Nick Flynn, Matthea Harvey,
Eileen Myles, D. A. Powell, and I wrote together, which
appeared in *Tin House*.

"Shakedown Machine" was awarded the Charles Angoff
prize from *The Literary Review*.

Big love to all of my friends and family—thanks for making this life possible. The good people of Milkweed Editions, Wayne Miller, Adam Clay, and Ada Limón—all of you rock and I love ya. A special thanks to TCU for the JFSRP Grant that helped support the completion of this book.

A.L.

ALEX LEMON is the author of *Happy: A Memoir*, and the poetry collections *Mosquito, Hallelujah Blackout,* and *Fancy Beasts*. His writing has appeared in *Esquire, Best American Poetry 2008, AGNI, BOMB, Gulf Coast, jubilat, Kenyon Review, New England Review, Open City, Pleiades,* and *Tin House*, among others. He was awarded a 2005 Literature Fellowship in poetry from the National Endowment for the Arts, and he contributes and reviews frequently for a wide range of media outlets. He lives with his wife and son in Fort Worth, and teaches at Texas Christian University.

Interior design and typesetting by Stewart A. Williams

Typeset in Excelsior